Animal Engineers

# SPIDERWEBS

by Nancy Furstinger

F⬤CUS
READERS

# FOCUS
# READERS

www.focusreaders.com

Focus Readers is distributed by North Star Editions:
sales@northstareditions.com | 888-417-0195

Produced for Focus Readers by Red Line Editorial.

Photographs ©: papkin/iStockphoto, cover, 1; Wolf Pictures/Shutterstock Images, 4–5; MarieAppert/iStockphoto, 6; QiuJu Song/Shutterstock Images, 8–9; PeteMuller/iStockphoto, 10; yod67/iStockphoto, 12; Rocket Photos/Shutterstock Images, 14–15, 29; Hafiez Razali/Shutterstock Images, 17; Marco Maggesi/Shutterstock Images, 19; Sarah2/Shutterstock Images, 20–21; Neil Bradfield/Shutterstock Images, 22–23; M_86/Shutterstock Images, 24; sarintra chimphoolsuk/Shutterstock Images, 26

**ISBN**
978-1-63517-863-0 (hardcover)
978-1-63517-964-4 (paperback)
978-1-64185-167-1 (ebook pdf)
978-1-64185-066-7 (hosted ebook)

**Library of Congress Control Number: 2018931117**

Printed in the United States of America
Mankato, MN
May, 2018

## About the Author

Nancy Furstinger is the author of more than 100 books. She has been a feature writer for a daily newspaper, a managing editor of trade and consumer magazines, and an editor at children's book publishing houses. She lives in upstate New York with a menagerie of animals.

# TABLE OF CONTENTS

# CHAPTER 1

# STICKY SPOKES

The sun has just come up. Dew sparkles on a spiderweb. A spider sits in the middle. She is waiting for her breakfast.

Suddenly a fly gets caught in her web. The spider rushes toward it.

 **A tiger spider catches an insect.**

Tiny drops of water can rest on a spiderweb's silk threads.

She bites the fly. Then she wraps the fly in silk. When the fly dies, the spider will eat it.

Spiderwebs can be many shapes. Each kind catches **prey** in a different way. Many spiders build orb webs. This kind of web is round. It looks like a bicycle wheel. The large outer circle has smaller circles inside it. Spokes run from the center outward. The web's sticky parts trap insects that fly by.

FUN FACT

An orb weaver builds a new web every night.

# CHAPTER 2

# BUILDING A WEB

A spiderweb is made of silk. It is made from strands of **protein**. The silk starts out as a liquid inside the spider's body. The spider **secretes** this liquid. Then the strands harden. They form thin threads.

**Spiders produce silk inside their bodies.**

A black widow spider has a red shape just in front of its spinnerets.

The spider weaves these threads together. To do this, it uses organs called spinnerets. A spider's spinnerets are on its stomach. The spider uses its legs to pull silk out from them.

Spiders can spin different kinds of silk. Some strands of silk are sticky. These strands help the spider catch food. Other strands are dry. They allow the spider to walk around on the web.

**FUN FACT**

Spiders have tiny claws on their legs. The claws keep spiders from getting stuck in their webs.

**A spider builds its web near a tree branch.**

Many spiders build webs in trees.

First, the spider climbs onto a

branch. Then the spider sends out a strand of silk. The free end catches on another branch. The spider attaches the silk to the first branch. Then it sends out more strands. These strands form a frame. The frame supports the rest of the web.

Next, the spider adds more dry threads. It starts at the outside of the web and works toward the center. A series of circles takes shape. Finally, the spider lays down a **spiral** of sticky threads.

# CHAPTER 3

# CATCHING PREY

Spiders are **predators**. They eat insects. Many spiders build webs to trap their prey. For example, orb spiders wait in the middle of their webs. Insects cannot see a web's thin silk. They fly into the web.

 **An oak spider sits in the middle of its web.**

The web's sticky strands trap the insects. They cannot get away.

The silk threads vibrate. The spider feels them shake. It knows something is caught in its web. Some spiders can also tell when things such as leaves get caught in their webs.

**FUN FACT**

Most orb web spiders have poor eyesight. They use their sense of touch to spin webs.

 **Spiders wrap their prey in silk.**

Most spiders spin their webs at night. Spiders usually work alone. However, some work together. They build giant webs. This helps them catch large amounts of prey.

Not all spiders spin webs. Instead, some go in search of their prey. Other spiders have different reasons for building webs. The

FUN FACT

Approximately half of all kinds of spiders spin webs.

 A nursery web spider makes a web shaped like a tent to protect her babies.

nursery web spider spins a web to protect her egg sac. The web acts as a blanket. The spider guards her eggs until they hatch.

# MANY WEBS

The shape of a web depends on the spider's **species**. Some spiders build webs shaped like **funnels**. The spider hides in the bottom of the web. It waits for prey to fall into the top.

Other spiders build loose webs in the corners of buildings. The webs use sticky threads to trap insects. If insects struggle, the threads pull them into the web's center.

Tiny spiders weave sheet webs. The webs are flat layers. The spider hides under the web. Insects fly into threads above the sheets. Then the insects fall onto the web.

Funnel-shaped webs are often found on the ground.

# CHAPTER 4

# PEST CONTROL

Spiderwebs help the **environment**. They allow spiders to catch large numbers of insects. Some of these insects fly through the air. Others live on the ground. Many are harmful pests.

**A golden orb spider traps insects in its web.**

 **A spider catches a grasshopper.**

For this reason, farmers welcome spiders into their fields. The spiders protect their crops. They catch bugs such as grasshoppers and beetles. These insects destroy plants. But one spider can eat approximately 2,000 insects in a year.

Without spiders, farmers would need to protect their crops in other ways. For example, they might use harsh sprays. Some scientists think humans might even face **famine**.

Spiders help indoors, too. They are useful to have around the home. Their webs catch harmful pests such as termites and roaches.

**Cellar spiders are commonly found in homes.**

Termites can destroy homes.

And roaches can carry disease.

Spiders also catch flies, fleas, and

mosquitos. These pests spread diseases to humans. Some of these diseases can be deadly. Without spiders, more families might use chemicals to kill these pests.

Many spiders are small. But they have a huge impact on the areas around them.

# FOCUS ON
# SPIDERWEBS

*Write your answers on a separate piece of paper.*

1. Write a sentence that describes the main idea of Chapter 4.

2. Which step of building a web do you think would be the most difficult? Why?

3. When do most spiders build their webs?
   - A. in the morning
   - B. in the afternoon
   - C. at night

4. What might happen if spiders stopped living in a field?
   - A. More sunlight could reach the plants and help them grow.
   - B. More insects could survive and eat the plants.
   - C. More water could stay in the soil for the plants to use.

**5.** What does **vibrate** mean in this book?

*The silk threads **vibrate**. The spider feels them shake.*

    A. move back and forth

    B. make a loud sound

    C. break into many pieces

**6.** What does **crops** mean in this book?

*For this reason, farmers welcome spiders into their fields. The spiders protect their **crops**.*

    A. tools that people use for farming

    B. harmful pests that eat leaves

    C. plants that people grow for food

*Answer key on page 32.*

# GLOSSARY

**environment**
The natural surroundings of living things in a particular place.

**famine**
An extreme shortage of food.

**funnels**
Tube-shaped objects that are wide at the top and narrow at the bottom.

**predators**
Animals that hunt other animals for food.

**prey**
Animals that are hunted and eaten by a different animal.

**protein**
A molecule that is important in telling a living cell what to do.

**secretes**
Releases something through the skin.

**species**
A group of animals or plants that are similar.

**spiral**
A line that makes a curving, circular pattern.

# TO LEARN MORE

## BOOKS

Furstinger, Nancy. *Spiders Are Awesome.* Mankato, MN: 12-Story Library, 2018.

Hayes, Amy. *Funnel-Web Spiders.* New York: Gareth Stevens Publishing, 2018.

Randolph, Joanne. *Orb-Weaver Spiders.* New York: PowerKids Press, 2014.

## NOTE TO EDUCATORS

Visit **www.focusreaders.com** to find lesson plans, activities, links, and other resources related to this title.

# INDEX

Answer Key: 1. Answers will vary; 2. Answers will vary; 3. C; 4. B; 5. A; 6. C